a potpourri of

PANSIES

Emelie Tolley and Chris Mead

CLARKSON POTTER/PUBLISHERS
NEW YORK

Copyright © 1993 by Emelie Tolley and Chris Mead, Inc.

Published by Clarkson N. Potter, Inc., 201 East 50th Street, New York, New York 10022. Member of the Crown Publishing Group. Random House, Inc. New York, Toronto, London, Sydney, Auckland

CLARKSON N. POTTER, POTTER and colophon are trademarks of Clarkson N. Potter, Inc.

Manufactured in Japan

Design by Justine Strasberg

Library of Congress Cataloging in Publication Data
Tolley, Emelie.
  A potpourri of pansies / Emelie Tolley and Chris Mead.—1st ed.
    p.   cm.
  1. Pansies.   2. Nature craft.   3. Cookery (Flowers)   I. Mead, Chris.   II. Title.
SB413.P2T65   1993
642—dc20   92-41125
                                                                      CIP

ISBN 0-517-59449-8

10   9   8   7   6   5   4   3   2   1

First Edition

To Albert Morris, a generous and good friend.
—ET

To my father, and to Barbara Brooks, who never gave up.
I'll miss them both.
—CM

Many people have helped us gather these pansies. We thank them all, especially Judi Boisson, Christina Borg, Joan Burstein, Susan Clapp, James Cramer, Alexandra Davis, Richard De Perro, Dorothy Devaney, Mary Emmerling, Sheila Guidra, Heard's Country Gardens, Jacqueline Horscher-Thomas, Dean Johnson, Irene Lord, Matthew Mead, Mario Montes, Janet McCaffery, Myra Oram, Kim and Ray Polley, John Reynolds, Jeremy Switzer, Martha Stewart, Barbara Trujillo, Whitmore's Garden Shop and Nursery, Polly Yuhas. Our appreciation, too, to Justine Strasberg for her sensitive design, and our friends at Clarkson Potter.

Introduction

It's hard to imagine anyone not liking pansies. With their pert little faces, velvety texture, and glorious colors, they enchant children and adults alike. Even those who are seduced by more sophisticated blooms reserve a special place in their hearts for the pansy's naive charm.

Pansies have been admired for thousands of years, from the time tiny Johnny-jump-ups grew wild in the fields, providing material for lovers' potions and medical cures and appearing as decorative garnishes at the table and in potpourris. In the mid-

Bonne et Heureuse Fête

19th century, they were hybridized to the large-flowered and varied plants familiar to us today, and pansy mania raged as they were grown for exhibition and prized as bedding plants. Victorian ladies adopted pansies with fervor and soon their pretty flower faces appeared in paintings and on china and other decorative objects. And since they represented "thoughts of you" in the language of flowers, their charming countenances on postcards and greeting cards carried a sweet reminder of affection to lovers and friends.

Although the mania for pansies abated in the early 1900s, they kept their place in many hearts and gardens. We are happy to see these appealing plants appearing once more in all their glory in gardens, in the kitchen, and as a popular design motif. In this little book we have gathered the very best examples of the pansy, both real and decorative, to celebrate its beauty and to bring joy to all those who love this beguiling little flower.

The Pansy

A SHORT HISTORY

The history of the common garden pansy is really rather short. While the irresistible Johnny-jump-up, the cheery little flower known properly as *Viola tricolor* because of its white, yellow, and purple petals, was transplanted to the garden from the wild long ago, it wasn't until the mid-1800s that the large, showy blossoms we know today came into being.

One of two English gardeners may have developed our modern pansy. Many credit Lady Mary Bennett, whose heart-shaped garden of heartsease drew the admiration of nurseryman James Lee. Her gardener and Lee's foreman experimented with hybridizing heartsease with a yellow-flowering perennial form of *Viola lutea* and a large blue viola from Holland.

At the same time a Mr. Thompson, gardener to Lord Gambier, was also working on a version that would have the charm of the wildflower but the size and beauty of a garden flower. By 1830 he had a large, beautifully shaped pansy rich in coloring with blotches on the petals.

Thompson passed his best varieties on to other growers resulting in a pansy craze that lasted from 1835 to 1838. The endless new varieties that resulted appealed to the Victorians, who adopted pansies as a decorative motif as well. Their popularity also encouraged unscrupulous growers to take advantage of the heightened interest to sell inferior pansy plants for very high prices. By 1845, however, things had settled down and a list of 354 different sorts of pansies appeared in a magazine of the time, *McIntoshes Flower Garden*.

Pansies became a florist's flower, grown for exhibition. From 1841 on, rigid rules defined the attributes of a show pansy: a nearly perfect circular shape with the lower petals making up nearly one half the flower; clear yet deep color; a well-defined margin and blotches. The eye had to be bright orange and clear-cut, not rayed or ragged. Needless to say, such pansies were difficult to cultivate.

Meanwhile, an Englishman named John Setter had imported the English pansy to

France from whence it traveled on to Belgium. Freed from his countrymen's exacting standards, Setter grew flowers that burst forth in gaudy colors with blotches on their petals. He triumphantly returned to England with his new pansy, which soon became known as the "fancy pansy." Although these brightly colored blooms were shunned by the upper classes for some time, they were adored by cottage gardeners and soon seen everywhere.

The same type of pansy came to America from Belgium in 1848 and enjoyed immense popularity here until the early 1900s. Wartime brought a temporary end to the pansy's reign because there was no time or manpower to continue the intensive hybridizing and cultivation of earlier years. Many varieties were lost forever. But sad as it may be to have lost these antique cultivars, many new pansies are being developed, and this enchanting flower is once more finding favor among gardeners and flower lovers.

11

What Is a Pansy?

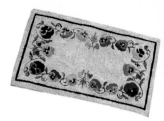

Since the garden pansy *(Viola x wittrockiana)* was bred from the original *Viola tricolor* and *Viola lutea*, all pansies are members of the Viola species, but not all violas are pansies. One major difference is that pansies generally have larger flowers but do not flower as profusely as violas. Violas are perennials while pansies, although they can be perennial under the right conditions, are more often treated as annuals or biennials.

The variety of different pansies and violas is staggering. Some pansies are true giants, with blossoms that can reach up to 4 inches. Violas are much smaller, going all the way down to the tiny Johnny-jump-ups. Both flowers, however, consist of five overlapping petals, each flower on a different stem. You can find blossoms in every color imaginable—blue, yellow, purple, lavender, rust, pink, orange, bronze, white, and even black—in single-color flowers as well as bicolored and tricolored ones. They may or may not have the blotches and rays that give them their "faces." Occasionally pansies have a lovely, lightly sweet fragrance.

12

The Decorative Pansy

Brightly colored and beautifully shaped, pansies are a favorite motif for decorative objects. In Victorian times they flourished on hand-painted china from France, Germany, and England, enhancing everything from washbowls and pitchers to tea sets, oil lamps, and vases.

Since then their cheery faces have been embroidered in silken threads on lace-edged throws, in bright cottons on white linen cloths, and in colorful wools on soft pillows. Pansies were scattered over fabrics; painted on velvet lingerie cases, calling card cases, and snapshot albums; hooked into rugs; and their likenesses adorned key holders and candy wrappers, porcelain pins, and velvet posies to decorate a dress or hat. These decorative pansies always provide a sense of pleasure.

A PANSY BOX

Using a variation on traditional découpage, any box can be transformed into a handsome container for potpourri, letters, or other treasures.

Select the box you want to decorate and cover the outside and the edges with two coats of acrylic paint. Assemble a group of greeting cards, seed packets, or magazine scrap and carefully cut out the pansies, including an occasional vase or pot for variety.

Arrange the scraps on the box with a temporary adhesive putty; it is often better to cut one picture into several parts and use the pieces on different sections of the box or to use extra leaves, flowers, or stems to fill in small holes. Affix the individual pieces with white glue, starting with those on the bottom layer; keep a barely damp paper towel or fine sponge handy to wipe up any excess glue. Use a small rubber roller or your fingers to press out any air bubbles under the scrap, then go over the edges of the paper with a burnisher to flatten them out and make the surface as even as possible.

After applying the entire design, allow it to dry thoroughly then cover it with several coats of matte latex polyurethane to which you have added a little raw umber acrylic paint. The umber will give the finished box a mellow antique glow. If desired, line the inside with a pretty paper.

A PANSY TABLE

A glass-topped table or tray provides a perfect ground for a decorative display of dried pansies. Though the pansies will fade if placed in direct sunlight, as their colors mellow they develop another kind of charm; if that's not to your liking, it's a simple matter to remove or replace them.

✻Remove the glass and working directly on the table surface, arrange the pansies in a border, an allover design, or overlap them for a lush look. Once the design is finished, attach the pansies to the tabletop with a small spot of white glue or a bit of double-faced tape. (If you plan to remove the pansies, use the tape as it will be easier to get them up.) Replace the glass over the pansies to protect them.

THESE Cupids are forging
a ring of gold
To send with my love;
if I'm not too bold.

Pansies in the Garden

The pansy's many-hued, velvety flowers add a note of joy to any garden whether they are bedded en mass as they were in Victorian England, circled around the trunk of a tree, tucked here and there in a border, or plopped into pots and window boxes.

Whether you buy plants from the nursery or start from seed, divisions, or cuttings, pansies are easy to grow. Bushy plants with healthy, dark green leaves can be successfully transplanted to the garden even when in bloom, but it's less traumatic for them if you remove all blossoms first.

Growing pansies from seed

offers the widest variety of color choices. In cool climates, sow the tiny seeds indoors in flats in late winter, covering them with ¹⁄₁₆ inch of soil, keeping them warm during the day and relatively cool (60–65° F/16–18° C) at night. Or, sow them outdoors in very early spring or in late summer for the following spring. Cover fall plants with a straw mulch thin enough to let the sun in. In milder climates, sow in late summer

or in early fall for winter blooms. Seeds germinate in one to three weeks. When seedlings are 2 inches tall, harden them off and plant them as soon as the ground can be worked. They will survive a light frost and some perennial violas bloom right through the spring snows—a truly cheery sight.

Since pansies are heavy feeders and can develop stem and root rot from standing in water, work a good all-purpose fertilizer or compost and some sand into the soil before planting to ensure ample nutrients and good drainage. Keep plants watered and feed well every few weeks for maximum bloom. Pinch back the stems regularly, limiting each plant to no more than six stems and dead head regularly before seed pods

form to encourage several months of large blossoms.

When the weather gets hot, however, most pansies flower less and eventually become leggy. When they begin to fade, cut the plants way back, feed them well, and as cooler days arrive, your reward will be vigorous new shoots and flowers.

Seeds gathered from your pansies will not necessarily come true, so propagate favorites by cuttings or division. In cooler climates, late summer is the best time to take cuttings. Cut a 2½- to 3-inch piece just below a joint on a young, vigorous stem; trim off the bottom leaves and any flower buds, leaving just a few leaves at the top. If the weather is warm enough, plant the cuttings 1½ inches deep and 8 inches apart directly in the prepared ground in a shady spot. If it's chilly, use a cold frame. Mulch well with compost to encourage new growth and pinch off the early buds to make the plant stronger. In cool climates, add a light straw mulch and they'll survive a winter where temperatures don't drop below 15° F/ − 9° C.

Divisions are equally easy and best done in spring or fall. Cut a sturdy plant into several pieces, each with some root attached, and replant immediately just as you would a cutting. Label them right away so you know what you have.

25

The Healing Pansy

Although *Viola tricolor* disappeared from pharmacists' books in 1926, it was once used as a blood-purifying agent for chronic skin complaints and rheumatism, as a diuretic, a tonic, a laxative, and to treat epilepsy, asthma, baby's skin diseases, and diseases of the heart. A simple infusion might have been prescribed as a gargle or a lotion to help heal wounds and sores, and a famous herbalist named Culpepper even recommended pansy syrup as a cure for venereal disease. This must have seemed logical if one subscribed to the school that like cures like: a pansy love potion might have been the cause of the disease.

A Bouquet of Pansies

No flower makes a more enchanting bouquet than the velvety pansy. It is possible to cut the stems long, but in doing so you lose many future pansies, so I limit the number of long-stemmed flowers I harvest. Put your pansies in a jug of cool water as soon as they are cut, and set them in a cool place for several hours before arranging them. The stems will absorb water and become more rigid and easier to work with. Pansy arrangements seem to look best in a rather short container with a narrow opening that allows you to mass them in clusters.

Place the shortest-stemmed flowers around the outer edge of the container, then pile the longer ones on top as you move toward the

center. An old-fashioned pansy ring will make your task simpler, and a really special bloom can be most appealing tucked in a small container all on its own.

Another possibility is to snip the blossoms off the stems entirely and float them on water in a pretty bowl for a marvelous mosaic that will last for several days. Massing two or three bowls of different sizes together produces a handsome centerpiece.

In choosing the pansies for an arrangement, I let my mood, the availability, and the container help me decide whether I will use subtle shades of one color, a harmonious mix of related colors, or a cheery melange of brightly colored blooms. The only thing that doesn't seem to work well for me is the combination of very pale pastels with their more gaudily colored relatives.

The Delights of Dried Pansies

ansies are among the easiest and quickest flowers to dry. You can enjoy their delightful faces on decorative candles, pretty lamp shades, colorful pictures, note cards or bookmarks, a bowl of lovely spring potpourri, or a decorative wreath.

Air-drying the flowers on a rack will give you multicolored puffs that are nice in potpourri, and the blossoms can also be pressed. But for lifelike versions that retain their color and shape, a chemical drying medium gives the best results. Spread a layer of silica gel in a large pan with a cover (I use a roasting pan) and lay the fresh pansies, with or without their stems, on top. Spoon another layer of silica gel over them, being careful to keep the petals flat, and cover. If the pan is deep enough, you can put several layers of pansies and gel in the same pan. Because the petals are so thin and fragile, they will probably be dry and crisp to the touch in twenty-four hours. Check by removing one flower from the gel. If it is not crisp, it will reabsorb moisture from the air and wilt; if it is overdried, it will be extremely brittle and the petals may shatter. Stored in an airtight box separated by sheets of wax paper and sprinkled with a little silica gel, pansies will retain their color for a reasonable length of time, especially if they are kept from severe humidity and bright light.

35

DECORATED CANDLES

Scented candles embellished with pansies make especially nice gifts. To make them, use white glue to affix dried pansies to candles in a pattern of your own design. Allow the glue to dry thoroughly. Place some paraffin in a tin can and set the tin in a pot of hot water over a medium flame until the paraffin melts. (Be careful; the paraffin is extremely flammable.) Holding the candle by the wick, dip it briefly into the melted paraffin. Let the paraffin harden for a minute or so, then repeat. The candle is now ready for use.

❋Note: If the candle is too tall to submerge completely in the paraffin, simply dip one half, turn it upside down, and dip the other end. There will be no visible line between the two halves.

I pray that you and care may never meet,
But here are purple pansies, fresh and sweet.

Cherish them tenderly, for, well we know,
Sure talismans are they 'gainst grief and woe;

Take, then, my pansies, that I bid you wear
Above your heart to ease its every care!

ANONYMOUS

LAVENDER PANSY BALLS

To make these colorful pomanders, cover a 2- or 3-inch Styrofoam ball generously with white glue and pat on a thick layer of dried lavender flowers. While the glue is still wet, press dried santolina flowers into the lavender in a widely spaced pattern, making sure they are flat against the surface. Using a small watercolor brush, carefully apply a thin layer of white glue to the backs of dried Johnny-jump-ups and press them onto the lavender among the santolina flowers in a pleasing pattern.

❋ On a larger ball you could use clusters of santolina flowers and full-sized pansies.

39

J. M. T Paris.

D
RECEVEZ mes Amitiés

SPRING POTPOURRI

I love to save the petals of all my spring flowers, spreading them out in patterned dishes to dry before turning them into a colorful potpourri. Pansies can be dried this way, too, producing fluffy little multicolored pieces. Since many of these flowers have no scent, I mix them with sweet-smelling dried herbs and oak moss that has been tossed with fragrant oil.

4 PARTS EACH DRIED NARCISSUS BLOSSOMS, DRIED GERANIUM PETALS, AIR-DRIED PANSIES, AIR-DRIED DELPHINIUM PETALS, AND BAY LEAVES

2 PARTS EACH DRIED WOODRUFF AND DRIED LEMON VERBENA

1 PART EACH DRIED ORANGE RIND, WHOLE CLOVES, OAK MOSS AND CORIANDER SEEDS

6 DROPS ROSE GERANIUM OIL, 4 DROPS BERGAMOT OIL, AND 2 DROPS CINNAMON OIL FOR EVERY ½ LB. (225 G) DRY MIXTURE

WHOLE PANSIES DRIED IN SILICA GEL

✳ Combine all ingredients except the whole pansies and allow to mellow in a tightly sealed jar for several weeks. Display in a bowl of your choice and scatter whole pansies on top.

Pansy Wreath

Dried herbs may be used for the base of this wreath, but fresh herbs are less fragile. If you can find marjoram, thyme, or mint in bloom, they look especially nice tucked in among the silvery herbs. Lay the finished wreath flat on a table until the herbs dry.

- Straw wreath form
- Silver King artemisia or other gray and green herbs
- A few sprigs of lavender or other purple-blossomed plants
- A selection of dried pansies
- Florist's wire and pins
- Hot-glue gun and glue

Place a large bunch of Silver King artemisia on the wreath form and wrap it securely with florist's wire. Make sure the bunch is big enough to spread out over the wreath and still look full. Attach a second bunch, overlapping and covering the stems of the first. Continue around the wreath, tucking the stems of the final bunch under the tops of the first. Next, wire together small bunches of the other herbs and, using florist's pins, attach them at intervals to add highlights. With a hot-glue gun add a few purple sprigs, then lots of different-sized dried pansies among the greenery.

What's in a Name

The jaunty Johnny-jump-up has more folk names than any other flower. Many of them reflect its long association with lovers or refer to its pert little face, including love-in-idleness, Cupid's flower, tickle-my-fancy, kiss-her-in-the-pantry (or buttery), heartsease, herb constancy, Jack-jump-up-and-kiss-me, kiss-me-quick, call-me-to-you, none-so-pretty, Kit-run-in-the-fields, monkey faces, peeping Toms, and three-faces-under-a-hood. In Denmark, Germany, and Scotland, pansies are sometimes called stepmothers: the large lower petal represents the mother, the middle petals her two daughters, and the two smaller petals at the top the stepdaughters.

The Painted Pansy

Among my favorite pansies are those that grow in my pansy paintings, many of them the work of Victorian ladies. I love to envision the ladies who painted them on a long-ago spring afternoon at a painting class, capturing the arrangement set out before them by the teacher. And it wasn't just an American phenomenon. When my great-grandmother emigrated from Belgium in the 1890s, she brought with her a painting of yellow pansies of the kind I now know were popular in France and Switzerland; and one of my favorite finds from the Paris flea market is an exuberant bunch of pansies depicted in a lovely rustic basket. I'm sure pansies have been a favorite subject of professional and amateur alike through the years because the urge to immortalize their fresh faces, rounded shapes, and mixtures of velvety color is irresistible.

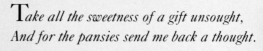

Take all the sweetness of a gift unsought,
And for the pansies send me back a thought.

SARAH DOUDNEY

A
PICTURE
OF
PANSIES

To create handsome pansy "prints," dry the pansies with their stems on or press the stems separately in a flower press. Leave any bends or twists in them; they add to the charm of the finished picture.

✳ Select a sheet of good artist's paper, preferably in an off-white shade, and lay the pansies out, moving them about until you create a pleasing design. Using different sizes and colors provides greater visual interest, but a mass of your favorite pansy could be equally appealing. Once the design is set, begin pasting it down. Start with the stems (if you have dried them on the flowers, snap them off before pasting them down), painting the backs with a little white glue and gently pressing them into place. Keep a barely wet paper towel nearby to wipe up any excess glue. Add the flower heads to the stems the same way. The finished "print" can be matted and framed.

Cooking with Pansies

I rejoice in the fact that pansies are both edible and decorative. Although only those with a perceptible fragrance have a pronounced taste, all of them are most enticing when used as colorful decorations for salads, cakes, cookies, and other foods. You can also float them in your favorite punch, trap them in ice cubes for cooling summer drinks, or freeze them in a block of ice around a bottle of vodka or white wine. One note of caution: Be sure any pansies intended for the table have been grown without pesticides which can be harmful if eaten. Before using, wash them under gently running cool water and carefully blot dry.

PANSY CHEESECAKE

This is a spectacular party dessert and, if you use a cheesecake from the bakery or the grocer's freezer, a snap to prepare.

2 CUPS (16 OUNCES) SAUTERNE OR OTHER SWEET DESSERT WINE
1 ENVELOPE UNFLAVORED GELATIN
1 9- OR 10-INCH CHEESECAKE, STORE-BOUGHT OR HOMEMADE
 FRESH PANSIES, WASHED AND DRIED

❋ Combine the wine and gelatin in a saucepan and let sit until the gelatin is dissolved, about 5 to 10 minutes. Place the pan over low heat and stir until the gelatin is completely melted and clear. Chill in the refrigerator or over a bowl of ice until the liquid becomes thick and syrupy.

❋ Spoon a thin layer of the chilled gelatin mixture over the cake and refrigerate until set. Arrange the pansies in an attractive pattern on top, pressing them lightly into the gelatin. Spoon another layer of gelatin on top and return to the refrigerator to set. Repeat until the pansies are completely covered. Keep refrigerated until serving time.

A PANSY ICE COOLER

Enclosing a bottle of your favorite vodka in a pansy-filled block of ice is both an attractive and practical way to keep the contents refreshingly cool. All you need is a half-gallon–size milk or juice carton, some fresh pansies, and water.

✻ Begin by cutting off the top of the carton, then set the bottle of vodka inside. Drop a few pansies into the carton all around the bottle and add an inch or so of water. Set the carton in the freezer until the water freezes. Repeat until the container is nearly full. Because the pansies float to the top, you must do this in layers. The final layer should be just enough water to cover any petals that are protruding. When you are ready to serve, peel the carton off and set the iced bottle on a deep plate or in a clear wine bucket that will catch any drips.

✻ A simpler version to embellish drinks can be made by freezing tiny Johnny-jump-ups in ice cubes. Or, if you are serving a punch, freeze pansies and water in a decorative mold, then float the beflowered ice block in the punch bowl.

56

Pansy Cookies

These charming cookies are not made with pansies, but have pansies painted on the icing. Since they are one of the easiest flowers to draw, don't be afraid to become a botanical artist next time you bake your favorite sugar cookies or gingerbread recipe.

Fondant Icing

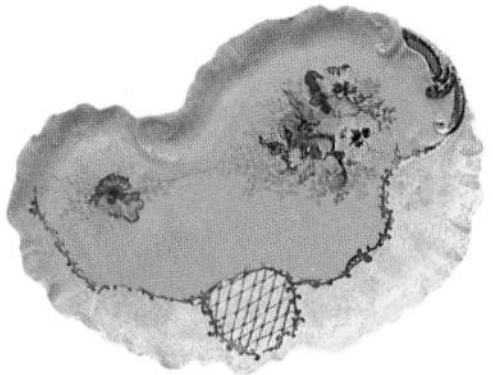

2¾ cups (550 g) granulated sugar
¼ teaspoon cream of tartar
Dash of salt
1½ cups (12 ounces) water
4 to 5 cups (550 to 750 g) sifted confectioners' sugar
½ teaspoon almond extract
Food coloring or icing gel

Place the granulated sugar, cream of tartar, salt, and water in a heavy-bottomed saucepan and mix well. Set the pan over a low flame and cook, stirring constantly, until the sugar is completely dissolved. Turn the heat up to moderate and continue to cook without stirring until a candy thermometer reaches 226° F/108° C. Remove the pan from the heat and allow it to cool until it can rest comfortably on the palm of your hand, or until the thermometer registers 110° F/43° C. Gradually beat in the confectioners' sugar, using only enough to make the icing the right consistency to spoon over the cookies. Just before using, stir in the almond extract.

✳Ice all the cookies and allow the icing to set. The surface should be
shiny and firm. Using food coloring (or icing gel dissolved with
a little water) and a fine brush, outline the shape of a pansy on
the face of each cookie in a pale wash of color or gray. Fill in the
petals with the colors of your choice. (Note: It is easiest to start the outline
with the bottom petal and work upward.)

Buisson

~Bonne et heureuse Fête~

pour souvenir Victor

The Loving Pansy

I *pray,*
what flowers are these?
The pansy this,
O that's for lover's
thoughts.

GEORGE CHAPMAN
"All Fools"

This unassuming little flower has been imbued with magical romantic powers, perhaps because the smiling faces brought to mind an absent lover. Whatever the reason, Celts brewed a love potion from the dried leaves while the smaller heart-shaped leaves were supposed to be capable of curing a broken heart. And when the knights of the Round Table wanted to forecast their romantic fortunes, they studied the rays on a pansy's face. Four rays signified hope; thick lines leaning to the left signaled a life of trouble; those leaning to the right, prosperity to the end. Seven rays brought constancy in love, and if the center line was the longest, a Sunday wedding was predicted. Eight rays foretold fickleness, nine a changing heart, and an unlucky eleven, disappointment in love and early death.